The Usborne Book of Animal Jokes

Designed and illustrated by Leonard Le Rolland

Edited by Laura Howell

Contents

A man went to see
the doctor one day
with a huge, fat
toad on his head.

My word!

...exclaimed
the doctor,

Where did that horrible
thing come from?

I don't know,

it started as a
wart on my bottom...

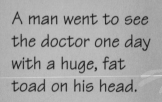

Slimy, Scaly and Slippery

You must be croaking!

What does a frog have with its burger?

Jumbo flies and a diet croak.

How does a frog feel when it has a broken leg?

Very unhoppy.

What kind of shoes do frogs wear?

Open-toad sandals.

What did the frog say in the library?
"Reddit... reddit... reddit..."

What's white on the outside and green on the inside?

A frog sandwich.

A frog went to see a fortune teller. She gazed deep into her crystal ball and said:

"Ah, yes... you will meet a beautiful girl, who will want to find out everything about you."

"That sounds great," said the frog. "Where will I meet her? By the pond? In the park?"

"No," replied the fortune teller. "In her biology class."

Rep-smiles

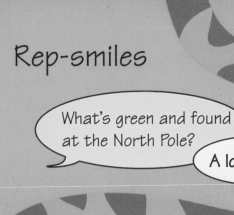

What's green and found at the North Pole?

A lost lizard.

What does a snake have for dinner?

Slither and onions.

What do you get if you cross a snake with a calculator?

An adder.

What does a Shakespearean snake say?

"To boa or not to boa, that is the question."

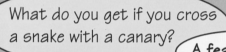

What do you get if you cross a snake with a canary?

A feather boa.

What do you call a snake on a building site?

A boa constructor.

What do you call an Arctic lizard?

An igloo-ana.

Why did the snake have a sore mouth?

There was a fork in his tongue.

Life in the ocean waves

What happened to the shark who ate a bunch of keys?

He got lockjaw.

What's the saddest creature in the sea?

A blue whale.

What do you get if you cross a jellyfish with a TV?

Jellyvision.

Did you hear about the baby octopus who disappeared?

He'd been squidnapped.

What kind of horse is best for playing water polo?

A seahorse.

What comes after a seahorse?

A D-horse.

Did you hear the joke about the electric eel?

It's shocking.

Why did the prawn never share with its friends?

Because it was a little shellfish.

Why do shellfish go to the gym?

To build up their mussels.

Slugs 'n' snails

Waiter, waiter! There's a slug in my salad!

I'm sorry sir, I didn't know you were a vegetarian.

What was the snail doing on the road?

About a mile a day.

Where would you find a crazy snail?

In a nut-shell.

What did the slug say when he left his friend's house?

See you next slime!

Make it snappy

What should you do if you find a crocodile in your bed?

Sleep somewhere else.

Knock knock.

Who's there?

Ali.

Ali who?

Ali gator bit my arm off – call an ambulance!

What do crocodiles use to grate cheese?

An ali-grater.

Why is a crocodile like a photographer?

They both snap.

How do you get a set of new teeth put in for free?

Annoy a crocodile.

What's got four legs and an arm?

A crocodile eating dinner.

A lady goes shopping one day and asks for some crocodile shoes. "Certainly, miss," says the assistant. "What size feet does your crocodile have?"

What do you call it when an alligator bares its teeth?

A croco-smile.

Something's fishy...

What kind of fish makes you an offer you can't refuse?

The Codfather.

What kind of fish can you keep on ice?

A skate.

Did you hear about the trout that taught itself to paint?

It had arty fishal intelligence.

Why are fish so clever?

They live in schools.

What kind of money
do fishermen make?

Net profits.

What kind of fish would
you find in a hospital?

A brain sturgeon.

What do you get if you cross
a shark with a cow?

I don't know, but I wouldn't
like to try milking it.

Why did the fish take
an aspirin?

It had a haddock.

Down on the Farm

One day, a farmer was milking his cow, when a fly flew into the barn.

It buzzed around the farmer's head a few times, then flew right into the cow's ear.

Mmmooooooo!

A few minutes later, the farmer was amazed to see the fly swimming around in the bucket of milk.

"Well, look at that!" he exclaimed. "It must have gone in one ear and out the udder!"

Fowl jokes

What do you call the door
to the chicken coop?
The hentrance.

Why do chickens like to
chat so much?

Because talk is cheep.

How do chickens like
to dance?

Chick to chick.

What do chickens use
to find things out?

A hen-cyclopedia.

The butt of the joke

What did the horse say to the goat?

"How are the kids?"

Knock knock.

Who's there?

Billy.

Billy who?

I can't billy-ve how long I've been waiting out here.

If milk comes from a cow, what comes from a goat?

Butt-er.

What do you call a goat who tells jokes?

Billy the Kidder.

Doctor, doctor! I feel like a goat.
How long has this been going on?
Since I was a kid.

Corny cows

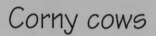

Why was the cow
unpopular in school?
He was a big bully.

Did you hear the joke
about the exploding cow?
It was a-bomb-in-a-bull.

What do you get if you cross
a cow with a vampire?

Something
terri-bull.

What do you get if you
cross a cow with a camel?
Lumpy milkshakes.

Did you hear about the cow who only ate money?
She produced rich milk.

What do you get from a nervous cow?

Milkshakes.

Where would you go to find a Russian bull?

Mos-cow.

What happened when the bull stopped shaving?

He grew a moo-stache.

What do you call a thief who steals cows?

Russell.

What happened when all the cows on the farm refused to be milked?

It was a moo-tiny.

How do cows get around?

By moo-torcycle.

Knock knock.

Who's there?

Cows go.

Cows go who?

No, cows go "Moooo!"

What do you call a scared bull?

A cow-ard.

Oinkcredibly funny

Why did the farmer call his pig "Ink"?

It kept running out of the pen.

What do you call a pig with no legs?

A groundhog.

What do you call a thief who steals pigs?

A hamburglar.

What has four legs and flies?

A pig.

What do police officers use when they arrest hamburglars?
Ham-cuffs.

What do you get if you cross Dracula with a pig?

A hampire.

What do you get if you cross a pig and a hedgehog?

A porkypine.

Why do pigs have two toes on each foot?

Because they'd look silly with two toes on their head.

What do you get if you cross a pig and a centipede?

Bacon and legs.

What do you call a ballet about pigs?

Swine Lake.

Why didn't the piglets listen to their teacher?

He was such a boar.

Where does a pig leave its car?

On a porking meter.

What club did the little pigs join?

The boy snouts.

What does a pig write at the end of a letter?

Hogs and kisses.

How do you describe an annoyed pig?

Disgruntled.

What do you call a pig with a car?

A road hog.

Did you hear about the pig that loved acting?

He was a real ham.

Horsing around

What do horses suffer from in the summertime?

Hay fever.

What do you give a pony with a cold?

Cough stirrup.

What kind of horse can never be ridden?

A clothes horse.

Where do you take a sick pony?

To the horsepital.

Did you hear about the really intelligent horse?
He was outstanding in his field.

Why did the man stand behind the horse?
He thought he might get a kick out of it.

Feeling sheepish?

Why did the sheep say "Mooooo"?

It was learning a new language.

What did the ram say to his girlfriend?

I love ewe.

What do you get if you cross a sheep with a lumberjack?

Lamb chops.

What do you get if you cross a sheep with a porcupine?

An animal that knits its own sweaters.

If one sheep is called a ewe,
what are two sheep called?
W.

Where do sheep go to get shorn?
To the baabaas.

Why did little Bo Peep
lose her sheep?
She had a crook with her.

What do sheep do
on a sunny day?
Have a baa-becue.

What sport are
sheep best at?
Baa-dminton.

Where do sheep go
in summer?
The Baa-hamas.

Pick
of the
Litter

Talking
dog
free to
good home

A man was walking down the street one day, when he saw a woman and a dog standing next to a sign:

Talking dog free to good home

Hey, dog!

...said the man.

Can you really talk?

"I certainly can!" replied the dog. "Not only that, but I was the first dog on the Moon. And I know the entire works of Shakespeare by heart."

"That's amazing!" remarked the man to the dog's owner. "Why would you give away a dog like that?"

I'm tired of his constant lies!

Cat's all, folks!

How would you describe
someone who's afraid of cats?
Pet-rified.

Did you hear about the cat that
entered the milk-drinking contest?
He won by six laps.

Why did the cat go to the doctor?
She was feline funny.

What do you get if you
cross a cat and a gorilla?
**An animal that puts
you out at night.**

What do you call a cat who does impressions?

An im-purr-sonator.

What do you call an accident-prone cat?

A catastrophe.

Is it hard to keep Oriental cats?

No, it's very Siameasy.

What kind of cat purrs the most?

A Purr-sian.

39

In the doghouse

What goes "Knock knock woof"?

A Labra-door.

Why do dogs lie down?
Because they can't lie up.

What do you get if you cross a Cocker Spaniel, a Poodle and a rooster?
A cockerpoodledoo.

What did the cowboy say when Lassie was kidnapped?

Well, doggone...

How do you describe a dog that won't stop chewing your furniture?

Very gnaw-ty.

What do you get if you cross a dog with a telephone?

A Golden Receiver.

Why did the man call his dog "Frost"?

Because Frost bites.

Why did the flea live on the dog's chin?

He wanted a woof over his head.

What's the difference between a police officer and a police dog?

The police officer wears a whole uniform, the dog just pants.

Watch the birdie

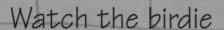

What do you get if you cross a canary with a Rottweiler?

Lots of very nervous cats.

What do you get if you cross a parrot and a hyena?

An animal that laughs at its own jokes.

What should you never do with a ten-ton canary?

Argue.

Tim: My canary died of flu.
Jim: I didn't know canaries got flu.
Tim: He flew into a closed window.

What do you get if you
cross a canary and a lawnmower?
Shredded tweet.

What kind of birds wore eyepatches
and terrorized Cornwall?
The Parrots of Penzance.

Why is a Spaniel like a parrot?
Because the Spaniel's a cockertoo.

Kid: Can I have a canary for Christmas?
Mother: No, you can have turkey like the rest of us.

Small and squeaky

Where do Dutch hamsters live?

In Hamster-dam.

What do you call it when two mice almost collide?

A narrow squeak.

How do you describe a really huge rodent?

Enor-mouse.

What's the difference between a cold and an escaped guinea pig?

You can catch a cold.

What's brown on the top, blue on the bottom and goes "Eeeeek!"?

A mouse sitting on an ice cube.

What do you call a really happy rodent?

A grinny pig.

What did the mother mouse say to her children?

"Squeak when you're squoken to!"

What do you call a long line of hamsters that can't move?

A hamsterjam.

No pet-ticular place to go

What do you call a stick insect with no legs?

A stick.

What do you get if you cross a goldfish and an ice cube?

A coldfish.

Why are goldfish like breakfast cereals?

They both come in bowls.

What do you get if you cross a Border
Collie with a Rottweiler?
A dog that bites your leg off then runs for help.

Knock knock.

Who's there?

Snakeskin.

Snakeskin who?

Snakeskin bite, so be careful!

What do you get if you cross a big dog
with a small rodent?
A Gerbil Shepherd.

I taught my canary
to play chess.

Wow, what a
smart bird!

Not really, I beat him
four times out of five.

Birdbrains

One day, a duck walked into a fancy department store and asked for some lipstick.

Certainly, miss!

...said the lady at the cosmetics counter.

And how will you be paying – cash or card?

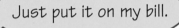

Just put it on my bill.

Don't get in a flap!

Why did the owl 'owl?

Because the woodpecker would peck 'er.

What goes "Hmmm-choo!"?

A hummingbird with a cold.

hmmm

I've had a parrot for ten years and it's never said a word.

Maybe it's shy.

No, it's stuffed.

What kind of bird is always making fun of people?

A mockingbird.

How does a chicken send a letter?

In a hen-velope.

mmmmchooO!

Knock knock.

Who's there?

Cook.

Cook who?

That's the first cuckoo I've heard this year.

What kind of bird has a shell?

A turtle dove.

When's the busiest time at a bird feeder?

Th'rush hour.

What kind of bird do you always find in the kitchen?

A cook-oo.

Did you hear the joke about the woodpecker?

It's boring.

What's pink and smells?

A flamingo eating garlic.

What kind of bird is always fooling around?

A lark.

What do you get if you cross a chicken with a centipede?

Enough drumsticks to feed an army.

Did you hear about the owl who lost his voice?

He didn't give a hoot.

What kind of bird can lift heavy weights?
A crane.

When's the best time to buy a canary?
When it's going cheap.

What kind of bird carries a pick and works underground?

A minah bird.

Watery birds

Why did the duckpond shake?

Because there was an earth-quack.

Doctor, doctor! I keep thinking I'm a duck.

Good, then you won't mind if I give you an enormous bill.

What happens when a duck flies upside down?

It quacks up.

What do you call a duck that chops down trees?

A lumberquack.

What do you sing to a duckling on its birthday?

"Happy birdie to you..."

If a swan sings a swan song, what does a cygnet sing?

A signature tune.

What do you call a failed pelican?

A pelican't.

Which seabird was a famous astronomer?

Gullileo.

Where do you go to see paintings of seagulls?

An art gullery.

Birds around town

Where do crows go for a drink?

A crowbar.

Why did the hen leap over the road?

She was a spring chicken.

What's black and white and goes round and round and round and round and round...?

A penguin trapped in a revolving door.

What kind of bird should you never take into a bank?

Robin.

Why did the bird sleep under the car?

To catch the oily worm.

A man walks into a police station with a penguin and says:

I found this penguin roaming the streets.

What should I do with it?

If I were you, I'd take it to the zoo.

The next day, the policeman's making his rounds when he spots the man walking down the street with the penguin.

Hey! Didn't I tell you to take it to the zoo?

I did. We're going to a museum today!

What's in a name?

What do you call a woodpecker with no beak?

A headbanger.

What kind of pie can fly?

A magpie.

What's big and white and sits in a tree in Australia?

A cooker-burra.

What do you get if you cross a bird with a bee?

A buzz-ard.

What's the definition of a greenfinch?

A goldfinch that isn't ripe yet.

Hey, that's not a bird!

What do you call a bat that performs somersaults in midair?

An acro-bat.

What's the best way to hold a bat?

By its handle.

What do you call a place for storing bats?

A battery.

How do you let a bat into your house?

Install a bat flap.

What kind of boat does a bat sail in?

A bat-amaran.

What's the friendliest kind of animal?
Bats, because they always
hang around together.

Why do bats use mouthwash?
They have bat breath.

What do you get if you cross
a bell with a bat?
A dingbat.

What do you get if you cross
a baseball player with a burglar?
Batman and Robbin'.

What did the toothless
vampire bat say?

Fangs ain't what
they used to be!

CREEPY CRAWLIES

One evening, a man was walking through town when he met a huge, ugly cockroach.

Before the man could say a word, the cockroach punched him and ran away.

Next day, the man's face was very sore, so he went to the doctor.

How did you get that black eye?

Well, you're probably not going to believe this, but I was punched by a giant cockroach.

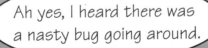

Ah yes, I heard there was a nasty bug going around.

Ants in your pants

What do you call an ant who's good at spotting things?

Observ-ant.

How would you describe an ant in a ballgown?

Very eleg-ant.

What do you get if you cross an ant with a mouse?

An ant-eek.

What do you call an ant who's good with numbers?

An account-ant.

What's the biggest kind of ant?

A gi-ant!

65

Oh, bee-have...

What do bees say in summer?

'Swarm.

What's another name for a bee?

A hum-bug.

What do you call a bee in a bun?

A hum-burger.

What band do bees like best?

The Bee-tles.

How do bees travel from city to city?
They catch the buzz.

What do you get if you cross a bee with a sheep?
A striped sweater.

What do you get if you cross a bee
with a book?
A sting in the tale.

THE
BEE-TLES

Why did the bee go
to Hollywood?

He wanted to be
in show bzzz-ness.

What musical instrument do bees play?

A hum-onica.

What did the bee say when it flew into a tornado?

"Well, I'll bee blowed!"

What does a queen bee do when she burps?

She issues a royal pardon.

What do you get if you cross a bee with a doorbell?

A humdinger.

What do you call an insect who's always complaining?

A grumblebee.

What kind of bee do you find in food?

Vitamin bee.

Knock knock.

Who's there?

Hive.

Hive who?

Hive been standing here for ages, let me in!

What country do bees like to visit?

Stingapore.

What do you get if you cross a bee with a deer?

Bambee.

Butterflies in your tummy

What do you get if you cross a
butterfly with a sack of potatoes?
Butterfries.

What did the caterpillar say
when he saw the butterfly?
**"You'd never get me up in
one of those things!"**

What do butterflies rest
on when they go to sleep?
A **caterpillow.**

What do you call a caterpillar that's
been stepped on by an elephant?

A flaterpillar.

What do you get if you cross a fly with a goat?
A butter-fly.

Why do butterflies drink nectar?
They can't open the ring-pulls on drink cans.

What do you call a dead butterfly?
A butterflew.

Did you hear about the caterpillar who wanted to make a fresh start?
He turned over a new leaf.

Why couldn't the butterfly go to the dance?
Because it was a moth ball.

Moth-eaten jokes

Why do moths have antennae?
Because they can't get cable TV.

What should you do if you find a drowning moth?
Give it moth-to-moth resuscitation.

Did you hear about the moth that
married the tablelamp?
It was love at first light.

What is a myth?
A female moth.

How does a moth feel when
it's been eaten by a bat?
Down in the mouth.

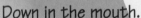

What do moths use
to play soccer?

A moth ball.

Doctor, doctor! I keep
thinking I'm a moth.

I'll be happy to help you,
just stop chewing on my ja

What insect lives
on nothing?

A moth, because it eats h

Why was the moth
so unpopular?

He kept picking
holes in everything.

What do you call a female moth
with lots of children?

A ma-moth.

Animal Crackers

One day, an elephant was taking a drink from the river, when he saw a turtle sitting on the bank.

He stomped over and kicked the turtle into the water.

Why did you do that?

...asked a passing monkey.

"That very same turtle bit my ankle 50 years ago. I recognized the pattern on its shell," replied the elephant.

What an incredible memory!

The monkey was impressed.

I know,

I've got turtle recall.

Funny bunnies

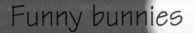

How do you stop rabbits from digging up your garden?

Hide the shovel.

Where do rabbits get their eyes tested?

At the hoptician.

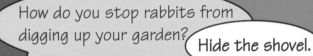

What do you call a rabbit that runs up and down the stairs?

A bunnister.

What's green, white and hops around?

A spring bunnion.

Just lion around

What do big cats
use to hang their
wet laundry?
A clothes-lion.

What do you call a
show full of lions?

The mane event.

What kind of cat should
you never believe?

A lyin'.

What does a lion use to
style his mane?

A cat-a-comb.

What does a lion say before it goes hunting?

"Let us prey."

How does a lion greet an antelope?

"Pleased to eat you!"

What happened to the cannibal lion?

He had to swallow his pride.

Knock knock.

Who's there?

Lionel.

Lionel who?

Lion'll eat you if you don't watch out.

If a four-legged animal is a quadruped and a two-legged animal is a biped, what's a tiger?
Stri-ped.

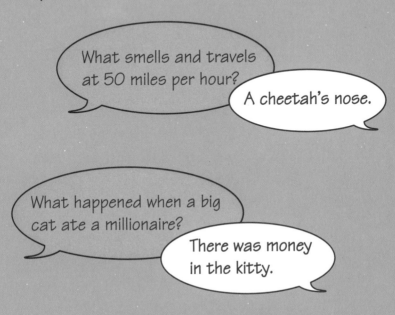

What smells and travels at 50 miles per hour?

A cheetah's nose.

What happened when a big cat ate a millionaire?

There was money in the kitty.

What do you get if you cross the American flag, a tiger and the lord of the jungle?
Tarzan stripes.

What do you call a tiger that's eaten your uncle's wife?

An aunt-eater.

Stripes...

If the dictionary goes from A to Z, what goes from Z to A?

A zebra.

Why are zebras black and white?

If they were black and yellow, you'd mistake them for bees.

What has six legs, four ears and stripes?

A girl riding a zebra.

What has sixteen wheels and stripes?

A zebra on roller skates.

...and humps

What do they sing in the desert at Christmas time?

"Oh camel ye faithful..."

What do camels use to wake up in the morning?

A llama clock.

What do you call a camel with three humps?

Humphrey.

Where did medieval people park their camels?

Camel-lot.

What has humps and can blend into the background?

A camel-eon.

Monkey business

What's the clumsiest kind of ape?

An orangutangle.

What do you call a monkey that can't keep secrets?

A blab-boon.

What kind of monkey would you find in a garden?

A chimp-pansy.

What do monkeys eat for dessert?
Ape-ple pie.

What do you call a crazy chimp?
A monkey nut.

How do you catch a gorilla?
Climb a tree and make a
noise like a banana.

Did you hear about the ape
who had a son?
He's a chimp off the old block.

How do monkeys make toast?
They put it under the g'rilla.

What kind of monkey floats through the air?
A baballoon.

Elephantastic!

What's big, wrinkled and has horns?
An elephant marching band.

What does an elephant wear to a wedding?
A tusk-xedo.

Why do elephants paint their toenails red?
So they can hide in a strawberry patch.

Why do elephants hide in strawberry patches?
So they can jump out and frighten people.

Kid: I have a really difficult homework assignment tonight. I have to write an essay on an elephant.
Dad: Well, you can borrow my ladder.

What has three tails, five ears and two trunks?
An elephant with spare parts.

What happened to the elephant
who ran away with the circus?
The police made him bring it back.

Can an elephant jump higher than a car?
Yes, cars can't jump.

What weighs four tons and wears glass slippers?
Cinderelephant.

What's big, carries a wand and gives
money to elephants?
The tusk fairy.

What do you call an elephant
who never takes a bath?
A smellyphant.

What's as big as an elephant but doesn't weigh a thing?
An elephant's shadow.

What do you call an elephant that can fly?
An elecopter.

Why do elephants have trunks?
They can't carry suitcases.

What's big and goes round and round?
An elephant in a washing machine.

92

What's big, wrinkled and mutters?
A mumbo jumbo.

What happened to the elephant who visited
a brewery?
He got trunk.

What game did the elephant play with the mouse?
Squash.

What's big and wrinkly and protects you
from the rain?
An umbrellaphant.

How do elephants talk
to each other?

By elephone.

Tail ends

What kind of animal falls from the sky?

Rain-deer.

What is Australia's most popular video game?

Mortal Wombat.

What lives in Australia and sticks its tongue out at people?

A kangar-rude.

Did you hear the joke about the emu?

It's very emu-sing.

What do lemmings like to drink?
Lemmingade.
What looks like a werewolf and goes "Squeak"?
A mouse going to a Halloween party.
Where do beavers keep their money?
In a river bank.
What kind of fur do you get from a skunk?
As fur away as possible.

First published in 2003 by Usborne Publishing Ltd.,
Usborne House, 83-85 Saffron Hill, London, EC1N 8RT, England.
www.usborne.com

Copyright © 2003 Usborne Publishing Ltd.

The name Usborne and the devices ♀ ⊕ are
Trade Marks of Usborne Publishing Ltd.

Printed in Italy